drawings by PHILIP MOOSE and KATE RUSSELL FORBES

EXPLORING THE COUNTRY INNS
of North Carolina

by
FARIS JANE COREY

THE PROVINCIAL PRESS   Box 2311   Chapel Hill, North Carolina   27514

Preface

Here are the country inns of North Carolina—those quaint retreats on "roads less traveled by" where guests may "sip, sup or bed." The hostelries usually reflect a rural, indigenous, homelike or oldtime appearance. Yet no place is alike another. One may have once been a rich man's grand estate. Or a less but still substantial country home. Another may have been a wayside inn, perhaps an early stagecoach stop, or a prominent village inn, set in the incomparable beauty of a small community like Hillsborough or Highlands.

Still, another could be a newer type of inn in North Carolina—the English-style "bed and breakfast." Retired couples and energetic housewives, for example, have converted into B&Bs such diverse facilities as grist mills, old schools, textile plants and family homeplaces. The conversions are almost a movement in some Tar Heel places like Asheville and New Bern where there are a number of bed and breakfasts.

Most of the establishments carry the word inn as part of their names. Some bear such synonyms as tavern, house, *manor, lodge* and more recently *bed and breakfast.* The names are interchangeable but have not always been so. In the early days of America the word *tavern* was generally used in New England while inn was more popular in Pennsylvania. The South favored the term *ordinary.* Some localities rejected *inn* as "too English." Following the American Revolution, *hotel* or *house* became more common in usage.

Like inns elsewhere in the country, those in North Carolina represent a time and place in the history of their location. Each in some way typifies its locale, people, style of living or even a past mode of transportation. The Henderson House at New Bern, for instance, mirrors the formal architecture of Pre-Revolutionary Governor Tryon's Palace. The Colonial Inn at Hillsborough the backwoods simplicity of early Piedmont. The Salem Tavern at Winston-Salem the craftsmanship of Germanic Moravian settlers.

The inns in this volume are truly rural (even though some are located in towns and cities), indigenous, historic or just quaint in character. Most provide overnight lodging—simple, clean, satisfying—and serve excellent food. A few, however, offer only one or the other. All comingle the past with modern comfort. Accommodations may not be stylish but neither are they dull with the sameness of a computer print-out. In fact, the individuality of the inns is the source of their distinctiveness. Each represents a gem to be discovered, enjoyed and treasured as a memory.

Revised 1987 by Jane Corey
ISBN 0-936179-08-2

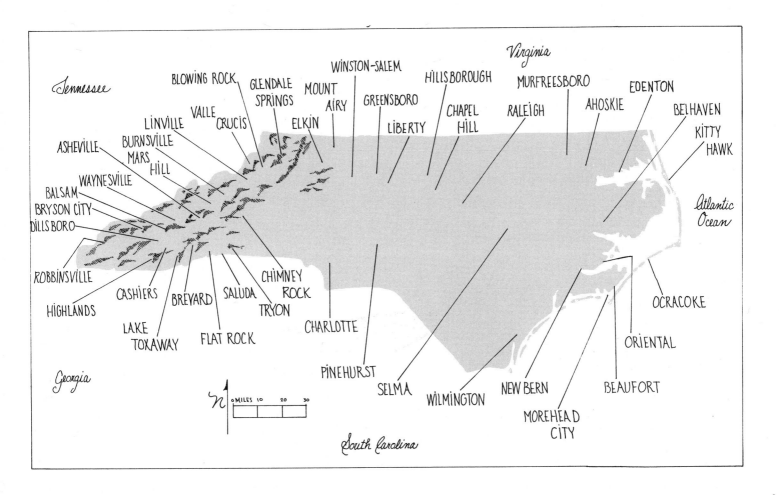

Contents

Grove Park Inn Asheville

Grove Park Inn, a monolithic structure of solid granite boulders topped by a red tiled roof, perches loftily above the mountain city of Asheville. Representing pre-1929 Asheville when the city boomed as a tourist resort, the 500-foot-long original inn sits stately amid quietly towering evergreens and is reminiscent of the gay days of the "Roaring Twenties." Its grandiose elegance contrasts sharply with the placid provincialism of smaller mountain inns.

The scenic drive to Grove Park ascends Sunset Mountain through a colorful residential section of spacious homes, many also of the 1920 era design. The drive ends at the imposing stone facade of the inn, through which guests move to the grand lobby or to a 200-foot rear terrace overlooking tennis courts and sloping fairways of a golf course. Asheville's skyline zigzags across the horizon beyond. Clearly seen, 30 miles away, is Mount Pisgah.

Grove Park Inn was erected in 11 months and 25 days, an astonishing feat in pre-World War I days. Native labor hauled stone boulders, some weighing five tons, to the building site. A train of 15 wagons pulled and steered by one motor truck transported over 40 tons of stone on a trip. Still covered by lichen and moss, the stone was laid on a steel and concrete frame.

Grove Park's 1913 opening was celebrated with an address by William Jennings Bryan. The famous orator and other men of comparable fame—Thomas Edison, Harvey Firestone, Henry Ford, President Woodrow Wilson and John D. Rockefeller typified clientele at the inn during its early days.

In fact, "prestige and relaxation" constituted keynotes of policy laid down by E.W. Grove in building the inn. The dream of Grove, owner of a pharmaceutical firm in St. Louis, was to erect in native stone a unique resort overlooking the mountains, a monumental landmark in his name which would be admired by generations.

Grove consulted many architects but none apparently grasped his idea. He then turned to Fred Loring Seely, his son-in-law and former Atlanta newspaperman, who proceeded to design without an architect and to build without a contractor a structure which came to be advertised as the "finest resort in the world."

The inn's large lobby, the Great Hall, is a favorite gathering place with its collection of comfortable antique furnishings, turn-of-the century atmosphere and massive fireplaces, large enough to burn 12-foot logs. The andirons weigh 500 pounds each. Engraved in the stone above are quotations from Ovid and Jefferson.

During World War II the United States government interred "Axis" diplomats from Germany, Japan, Italy and other enemy countries at Grove Park Inn. Later, the U.S. Navy leased the facility as a rehabilitation center for Naval officers.

In 1955 a Dallas firm bought and enlarged the vintage facility to include a 200-room wing, blending gracefully into its Sunset Mountain site. Further additions in subsequent decades include other wings, the adjacent country club, indoor tennis courts and swimming pool, five restaurants and horse drawn carriage rides.

The additions in their way are as impressive as the original structure. The address: The Grove Park Inn and Country Club, 290 Macon Avenue, Asheville, NC 28804. Telephone: 1-800-438-5800.

Balsam Lodge Balsam

A railroad depot and a nearby yellow clapboard house which once accommodated guest overflow at the old three-story wooden hotel named the Balsam Lodge now combine as the new Balsam Lodge. The hotel burned in the early 1970s and was not replaced. A couple from North Adams, Massachusetts, Gordon and Marie Pike, put the hotel's backup facilities into operation.

The depot, built in 1908 when the railroad from Murphy to Balsam was completed, divides into four bedrooms. In one room, the ticket booth, is a bay window. The yellow clapboard house, built in 1906, also has four bedrooms along with a gingerbread porch, wooden swing and hummingbird feeder. It overlooks a small pond with a waterwheel.

Breakfast is a special affair in the living room with ruffled curtains, chintz couches and tables set with white cloths and fresh flowers. Homemade biscuits, muffins and other breads hot out of the oven; preserves, jams and jellies; and steaming coffee headline the menu.

The Balsam Lodge season runs from spring flowers (June 1) to autumn leaves (November 1). The telephone: (704) 456-6528. The address: Box 279, Balsam, NC 28707.

Weaverville Milling Company Restaurant Weaverville

The main building of Weaverville Milling Company on Reems Creek Road outside Weaverville operated from 1912 to 1965 as a grist mill. In 1981 Sally and Kevin Smith opened it as a restaurant. Kevin's engineering skills helped make the change.

The interior today reflects an interesting and authentic picture of an operating mill of the early 1900s and diners enjoy it as well as the good food. The dining rooms with high ceilings occupy the main floor of the mill. Tables are spaced in and among the various milling machines. No part of the water-powered machinery remains, however.

The menu includes such classic stand-bys as prime rib of beef, veal florentine and fresh trout.

There is no lodging.

A small craft shop sells quilts and local crafts.

The address: Weaverville Milling Company Restaurant, Reems Creek Road, Weaverville, NC 28787. Telephone: (704) 645-4700.

Ragged Garden Inn and Restaurant Blowing Rock

The Ragged Garden Inn and Restaurant occupies a majestic house built in 1900 on a full acre lot in Blowing Rock, a "summering hole" in the mountains for four generations of Southerners. Locals describe many of the families as wealthy who "passed through and left a touch of their gold along with their memory."

Joe and Joyce Villani converted the summer house of one such family into an exquisite bed and breakfast called the Ragged Garden. It is a special chestnut bark covered place on a knoll overlooking a green lawn. Guests enter the yard through a gate flanked by two stone pillars. A wooden fence extends from the gate with roses threading thorough the rails. The inn sign is custom painted in blue and green and illustrated in style of the English inn.

Lodging consists of six rooms, one being a loft and the other a suite. They are tastefully decorated, immaculately clean. A delightful continental breakfast is served on the terrace, weather permitting.

The Villanis opened their place in 1982, first as a restaurant (the rack of lamb is recommended), and then they "sort of fell into running an inn."

Happenstance or not, the Ragged Inn is distinct.

Both the inn and restaurant are opened from April 15 to November 15. The inn continues through winter but the schedule of the restaurant is modified. Patrons are advised to call for winter opening dates.

The address: Ragged Garden Inn and Restaurant, Box 1927, Sunset Drive, Blowing Rock, NC 28605. Telephone: (704) 295-9703.

Hound Ears Lodge Blowing Rock

Hound Ears Lodge is part of a 900-acre luxury mountain resort. From Blowing Rock and Highway 105 the retreat is reached by the winding Shull's Mill Road. Its name comes from a rock formation known as "Hound Ears," an area landmark for generations. The lodge, club and golf-tennis-ski facilities were built in 1962.

The lodge houses 50 guests, who enjoy club privileges. Rooms have balconies. Gourmet dinners are served in two dining rooms.

The Hound Ears' address: Box 188, Blowing Rock, NC 28605. Telephone (704) 963-4321.

Green Park Inn Blowing Rock

Green Park Inn straddles the Eastern Continental Divide of America. Rain water from the front of the lodge flows north to the New River, then to the Ohio and Mississippi, and finally to the Gulf of Mexico. A spring near the southern end of the inn drains into a stream which empties into the Yadkin River and eventually the Atlantic Ocean.

The geographical location has long made Green Park a popular inn. Since its opening in 1882 guests have enjoyed spectacular views from the Blowing Rock across the road. They have also liked the embracing air of Green Park's 4,200-foot elevation.

Lenoir investors headed by G.W.F. Harper, a Civil War veteran active in furniture manufacturing, financed construction of the Green Park. Members of the Green family furnished the land, helped build the inn and for many years maintained it. The landmark was named for them.

In early days the white clapboard lodge was reached partly by railroad to Lenoir, 18 miles away. Horse-drawn surreys and baggage wagons hauled guests the final stretch up the mountain to the inn.

In 1952 J.E. Broyhill of Broyhill Furniture Company bought the Green Park. In 1977 Harry Robbins of Blowing rock acquired the old-timer and he in turn sold it to Ben Douglas, Jr. of Charlotte and Joe Mertes of Winston-Salem. Allen and Pat McCain, owners of a Vero Beach, Fla., hotel bought the inn in 1982. They continued the previous owners' tradition of providing both modern conveniences and old-fashion charm and individuality. Especially nice are the slowly turning ceiling fans, inside wicker furnishings, wicker rockers on the veranda, and leaded glass windows in the terraced dining room epitomizing the unstated intricacy of the inn's Victorian architecture.

Opened May through December, the Green Park lives on as a grand old mountain inn with distinctive class.

The Green Park address: Box 7, Blowing Rock, NC 28605. Telephone: (704) 295-3141.

The Inn at Brevard

Brevard

The Inn at Brevard, an elegant dining and lodging retreat in the "Land of Waterfalls," was built at the turn of the century as the home of famed attorney and mayor of Brevard, William E. Breece. In 1911 he hosted a reunion of troops who served under Confederate General Stonewall Jackson.

In 1984 Bertrand and Eileen Bourget acquired the Colonial-style historic facility and named it The Inn at Brevard.

They offer four bedrooms in the main house and ten in an adjacent lodge. Full breakfast comes with the tariff.

Lunch and dinner are served in the main dining room (also opened to the public). An executive dining room is named for General Jackson.

The address: 410 East Main Street, Brevard, NC 28712. Telephone: (704) 884-2105.

Fryemont Inn Bryson City

Fryemont Inn, lodged on a mountain shelf within walking distance of downtown Bryson City, was constructed by lumber baron Captain Amos Frye early this century. Frye built it to last. He had the exterior shingled with poplar bark, furnishings fashioned out of cherry and walnut woods, doors grooved with ornamental hardware forged by a local blacksmith, floors covered with hardwood and enormous fireplaces constructed in the lobby and dining room by Cherokee stonemasons. He faced each of the inn's 37 rooms either toward woods or the distant Great Smoky Mountains. He cut trails to Deep Creek, where, ten minutes away, cold water tumbles through forests.

Through the years cooking became lavish at Fryemont with fresh biscuits and a nutty cheese soup becoming popular, standard fare.

The inn ranks as a distinctive Tar Heel rustic, having operated continuously since 1923 except for a time in the late 1940s and early 1950s. It is listed in the National Register of Historic Places. Proprietors since Frye's death include his wife, a Cullowhee contractor and daughter, and George and Sue Brown who took over in 1982.

The Browns have continued the Fryemont in the tradition described by Samuel Johnson in 1776:

> There is nothing yet been contrived by man
> by which so much happiness is produced as
> by a good tavern or inn.

The inn is opened May through November. The address: Box 459, Bryson City, NC 28713. The telephone: (704) 488-2159.

Randolph House Bryson City

Timber baron and attorney Amos Frye built "The Mansion" in 1895 from select hard woods. He peaked the large roof with 10 gables and cut 50 windows to admit plenty of light. The mansion has been a country inn since 1923 with John Randolph as first innkeeper. The inn continues to bear his name and a niece Ruth Randolph Adams and her husband Bill carry on his tradition of hospitality.

Randolph House offers six bedrooms containing some of the original furnishings, pedestal sinks and claw-footed tubs.

Two meals, breakfast and dinner, are served daily in the dining room or on a terrace to overnight guests and by reservations to the general public. Guests may relax on the porch in country rockers. On chilly evenings they can enjoy a blazing fire in the large open fireplace.

Randolph House is opened April through October. The address is Fryemont Road, Box 816, Bryson City, NC 28713. Telephone: (704) 488-3472.

Hemlock Inn Bryson City

Hemlock Inn sits on a small mountain overlooking three valleys and distant misty peaks. There's little noise except that of lyrical birds. Meadows are agleam with wildflowers as far as the eye can see.

Hiking, shuffleboard and ping pong are the sports around the Hemlock. Two miles of trails lace through the 65-acre wooded tract owned by Innkeepers John and Ella Jo Shell, formerly of Marietta, Georgia. Fishing is popular, too, with rainbow and brown trout stocked in nearby Deep Creek.

Meals are family-style, served on bountifully set Lazy Susan Tables. Fried chicken, country ham, fresh vegetables, homemade breads and other robust foods native to the mountain region are standing fare.

The Shells are the third owners of the country inn built in 1952, one mile off Highway 19, three miles north of Bryson city.

After 30 years of swapping recipes with guests on a one-to-one basis, the innkeepers have written them down and told the story of Hemlock Inn in a cookbook, *Recipes From Our Front Porch* ($10 postpaid). Prospective guests learn much about the inn and environs by ordering the book prior to their visit.

The Hemlock Inn address: P.O. Drawer EE, Bryson City, NC 28713. Telephone: (704) 488-2885.

Celo Inn Burnsville

Randall and Nancy Raskin continue the legacy of Charles F. and Susannah Jones who created Celo Inn near Burnsville with rustic simplicity of design, attention to detail, hand labor and the use of native hemlock, oak and pine. The inn represents the creation of a building which "harmonizes with mountainous beauty of the Blue Ridge."

The retreat sits in a valley at the foot of the Black Mountains, the highest of which is Mount Mitchell. It blends with the stunning mountains which backdrop forests, meadows and hay fields and creeks. The South Toe River tumbles through the valley floor.

The five-room inn operates as a privately owned venture on land leased from the Celo community. Celo is an "intentional community," where land is group owned. Families and businesses hold leases on the land but cannot sell the land or renovate structures without group permission.

About 32 familes live in the Celo community on 1,210 acres straddling Highway 80. Businesses, in addition to the inn, include a summer camp for children, a progressive boarding school for grades seven to nine, a health center, a cooperative food market and the Toe River Cooperative.

Quaker philosophy, because of social idealism it imparts, underlies the community makeup. Actually the American Friends Service Committee helped found and still helps govern Celo. Less than a third of members are Quakers, however.

Celo was established in 1937 as a utopian experiment in community living, advanced farming techniques and group ownership. The idea was that of Arthur Morgan, a civil engineer, president of Antioch College and chairman of the Tennessee Valley Authority.

Because of the heritage Celo Inn reflects as part of one of the oldest continuing community enterprises of its kind, the inn is a special treat. Add to that its services and mountain setting and the treat is double. The telephone is (704) 675-5132. The address: 1 Seven Mile Road, Burnsville, NC 28714.

Nu-Wray Inn Burnsville

Few road signs lead the traveler to the Nu-Wray in Burnsville. But once in the mountain town, the visitor will have no trouble finding the place if he or she will go directly to the village green and follow the smell of good food.

The inn is a handsome dwelling, looking just like an inn should look on a village square, and is one of the few old-time country inns remaining in the region.

Its bountiful, family-style meals are veritable feasts. Platters and bowls are passed from guest to guest at long well-appointed tables in the comfortable dining room. Practically everything from the kitchen is homemade. Mountain cabbage leave the chopping block as crisp chow-chow. Tiny sugar pumpkins come out as spicy pumpkin pies and plain dried beans as richly baked beans. Mountains of steaming cornbread, along with candied yams, corn pudding and tangy cranberry salad, crowd the table. Cooked apples appear as glazed stack cakes.

The inn once served three meals a day but several years ago reduced them to two—breakfast (8:30) and supper (6:00), except on Sundays and holidays when breakfast and lunch (1:00) are served. A clanging bell at 8 a.m. alerts guests that breakfast will be served within half an hour.

Established in 1833, the inn has provided generations of travelers with a bright fire, warm food and lodging for the night. Following the naming of Burnsville as the county seat of Yancey County, the inn became a special staying-over place for traveling judges and lawyers until terms of court ended.

In 1870 Garrett D. Ray purchased the inn and enlarged it. His daughter Julia married William B. Wray of Shelby, who in 1918 changed the name to Nu-Wray. A fourth generation of the family continues its operation.

From the lobby through the halls to the bedrooms, relics of over a century abound. There are spinning wheels, grandfather clocks, sculptured pianos, coffee grinders and unadorned wrought iron beds. Old pictures, including 19th century pastorals, line the walls. An aged reproduction of a picture of Robert E. Lee and Stonewall Jackson graces the dining room. And, of course, Nu-Wray Inn itself is a picture. With its white coat of paint and black shutters and flanked by a small garden, the local institution is quite a handsome sight on the village square.

The Nu-Wray address is Box 156, Burnsville, NC 28714. Telephone: (704) 682-2329.

High Hampton Inn Cashiers

High Hampton Inn, like most country inns, appeals to those who prefer simplicity, natural beauty and tradition. It began in storied Cashiers Valley as the private summer home of the distinguished South Carolina Hampton family. Famous Southerners like John C. Calhoun visited the mountain retreat for hunting, fishing and cool climate.

General Wade Hampton acquired the estate prior to the Civil War. The "Giant in Gray" came to it for rest and relaxation, brought trout fingerlings to the streams and planted fruit and vegetable gardens. He named the huge farmhouse High Hampton. After the war the General freed his slaves and left his "Millwood" plantation near Columbia, S.C. which had been pillaged by Sherman's Army. Hampton moved to the Cashiers estate which he said would provide peaceful plenty for his then poor family.

A niece of General Hampton, Caroline, lived on the estate but impoverished conditions in the South caused her to go to Baltimore where she became head surgical nurse at Johns Hopkins Hospital. There she married Dr. William S. Halsted, then chief of surgery. They spent their honeymoon in 1890 at High Hampton.

Dr. Halsted liked the estate, purchased it from Wade Hampton's sisters and made it a center for medical consultation, attracting doctors worldwide. They came to relax and consult with him. He had conceived and put into operation aneurysm surgery, developed use of rubber gloves in surgical procedures, discovered local anesthesia and worked out a system of gall bladder surgery.

Following the death of Dr. and Mrs. Halsted in 1922, the property was purchased by E. Lyndon McKee, president of the Sylva Paperboard Corporation. In 1923 McKee and his wife opened a small inn and named it High Hampton Inn. The Swiss architecture and bark exterior reflected an early mountain living style.

The McKees' son, William D., continued the inn's operation. In time about 50 private homes were built around it.

Although outsiders are welcomed to High Hampton, opened May through October, the inn is essentially a family resort. The same families, generation after generation, come to it for reunions.

The address: High Hampton Inn and Country Club, Cashiers, NC 28717. Telephone: (704) 743-2411.

Esmeralda Inn Chimney Rock

Esmeralda Inn, near Chimney Rock park, opened in 1892. Colonel Tom Turner of New York built the first structure which reached a peak of popularity in days of the silent motion pictures. Such films as "In the Heart of the Blue Ridge" and "The Battle Cry" were filmed in surrounding mountains and the film companies lodged at the Esmeralda. Local people appeared in bit parts.

The original inn burned in 1917. The new structure with 15 guest rooms was quickly constructed, centered by a massive stone fireplace, which the 30-foot ceiling almost dwarfed.

The lobby is unique with natural trees and limbs creating a wrap-around balcony.

A menu of fresh "country gourmet" served in the dining room or on one of the covered verandas attracts people from miles away.

Pete and Pam Smith, formerly of Atlanta, bought the inn in 1983 and serve as the innkeepers.

Opened from late March through early November, the Esmeralda sits off Highway 74. The address: Box 57, Chimney Rock, NC 28720. Telephone: (704) 625-9105.

Jarrett House, Dillsboro

A wide porch with latticed banisters and rocking chairs fronts each of the three floors of the Jarrett House in the mountains of western North Carolina at Dillsboro. From the porches guests can rock and view across the road the rapid Tuckaseigee River spill over a small power dam and bend sharply on its way to nearby Fontana lake. When foliage permits, guests also can see the quaint Riverwood Craft Shop on the far bank of the river where craftsmen turn out hand-wrought pewter ware, enameled copper and woodcarvings.

Inside the white frame Jarrett House the guests enjoy food in a dining room featuring a large window overlooking a lovely mountain garden profuse with rock boulders, laurel, ferns and mimosa. The room is redolent with the scent of good cooking mingling with the smell of the aged wood of the 19th century inn. Freshly cut flowers in season on each of the dining room tables complement the outside garden greenery.

Mountain trout and country cured ham are traditional Jarrett House dinners. These and other entrees are served family style on large platters accompanied by briming bowls of home-grown beans, corn, tomatoes, okra and apples. Waitresses continually replenish the hot biscuit bowl.

Nineteenth-century decor extends throughout the interior. The parlor, a victorian replica, for example, includes corner cupboards, plank floors, lace curtains, an aged piano and other period pieces.

The Jarrett House is the focal point of the small village of Dillsboro, which began years ago at the point where construction of the railroad into the area was halted because of a mountain barrier. While crews bored a tunnel through the mountain, W.A. Dills laid out a community, named it for himself and sold lots. He also built the Jarrett House. Erected in 1884, it was first named Mount Beulah Hotel for Dill's youngest daughter. Its present name honors R. Frank Jarrett, who bought the inn in 1894 and renamed it Jarrett Springs Hotel. A subsequent owner shortened the name in 1950 to Jarrett House. Jim Harbarger and wife Jean and two sons purchased the Jarrett House in 1975 and continued the operation offering both meals and lodging.

The address: The Jarrett House, Box 219, Dillsboro, NC 28725. Telephone: (704) 586-9164.

Squire Watkins Inn Dillsboro

Squire Watkins Inn features a Victorian-style farm home with handsome woodwork, antique furnishings and two porches (lower and upper floors) for rocking. There are five bedrooms, one with a separate sitting room. A special Squire's breakfast comes in a formal dining room.

The house was built by J.C. and Flora Zachary Watkins, who married in 1880. Watkins was a devout Baptist, a merchant and magistrate. During his 16 years on the bench, he never had a decision reversed. Among the first settlers in Dillsboro, the couple erected the large home overlooking Dillsboro. It was patterned after the childhood home of Flora, who was the well-educated granddaughter of the founder of the nearby resort Cashiers. J.C.'s untimely death left Flora to raise their large family alone. She supported them by opening the house to boarders.

Descendants of the family lived in the house until 1983 when it was purchased by Tom and Emma Wertenberger. They turned the dwelling into an attractive bed and breakfast and continued to connect it with the Watkins family by naming the enterprise Squire Watkins Inn. It is opened year round. The telephone: (704) 586-5244. The address: Box 430, Dillsboro, NC 28725.

Woodfield Inn Flat Rock

Woodfield, the oldest continuously operated inn in North Carolina (1850), reflects the luxury of its eventful past. Its many rooms house a treasury of antiques. In the hallway stands a corner cupboard in use since 1852. The shelves are stacked with original dishes of the inn. Four 1742 Hogarth engravings hang in the Georgian living room. A Grandfather clock over 400 years old ticks away in the reception room. Black walnut mantels frame fireplaces in 22 rooms.

A wide piazza shades the front of the building. Wooden pegs hold together the structure's hand-hewn foundation. White pine covers the exterior and oak the interior. Multi-hued handblown glass panes remain intact as well as gold brass hardware pieces.

Woodfield Inn was built in 1850 by a group of Southern leaders headed by William Aiken, then governor of South Carolina. In 1853 H.T. Farmer bought the inn, named it Farmer's Hotel and operated it until his death in 1883. During the last six months of the War Between the States, Flat Rock citizens feared renegade lawlessness. A company of Confederate soldiers, commanded by Captain B.T. Morris, took post at the hotel to protect the community.

Following the war the inn became the social center of Flat Rock, often called "provincial Charleston." Also, it was the first stage coach stop south of Asheville and passengers put up there for the evening. They would sit around the roaring fires and trade travel experiences before retiring.

The tradition of good service, food and facilities provided so well and so long by Farmer was continued by a Miami couple, Mr. and Mrs. Joseph N. Clemmons, who bought the property in 1939 and operated it as Woodfield Inn for 30 years. Subsequent owners renovated the landmark. Although the name and owners of the inn have changed, the antebellum Southern ambience has not since its 1850 beginning.

The Woodfield address: Box 96, Flat Rock, NC 28731. Telephone: (704) 693-6016.

Glendale Springs Inn and Restaurant Glendale Springs

Glendale Springs Inn and Restaurant claims as its essence feasting in simple elegance and sleeping in country comfort. The feast is based on a French-inspired menu, baked goods from the in-house bakery, ice cream made in the kitchen and flowers, herbs and vegetables grown in the inn garden. There are bedrooms filled with country antiques, quilts made by Innkeeper Gayle Winston's mother, great-grandmother and Aunt Allie, and rugs hand-hooked by Aunt Carrie. There are private baths but no television or telephone.

The three-story Queen Anne-style house was built in the 1890s by General John Adams. Before Mrs. Winston bought the dwelling in 1980, it had served as a wayside inn, spa, public meeting house, store, dance hall, rooming house and WPA (Works Progress Administration) headquarters during construction in the 1930s of the Blue Ridge Parkway which passes 300 yards away.

Further complementing the inn's country motif are wide verandas, upstairs porches, hand-hewn pilings, yellow pine floor boards, wormy chestnut paneling, poured glass windows and carbide gaslight fixtures.

"Add to that the occasional ghost story and my childhood memories of the biggest house I had ever seen," says Mrs. Winston.

"When it was offered at auction, how could I resist?"

Within sight of the inn is Holy Trinity Episcopal Church, well-known for frescoes by artist Ben Long. Nearby is New River where guests may canoe.

The address: Glendale Springs, NC 28629. Telephone: (919) 982-2102.

C. DICKINSON

Highlands Inn Highlands

Highlands Inn, an old-timer with porches running the length of its first and second levels, occupies the prominent corner of the mountain village Highlands. The inn has been a landmark since stagecoach days of 1879 when Joseph Halleck built it with virgin timber and handmade nails. The facility operated for three years as Highlands House. The name changed to Smith Hotel with purchase by John J. Smith and during the Depression to Highlands Inn with purchase by Frank Cook. Helen Major managed the facility for many years before passing control to Glenn and Shan Arnette, purchasers in 1983. They in turn sold to E.W. Hood in 1986.

The Arnettes and Hood rejuvenated the "old girl" but carefully retained its historical elegance and general character. They enjoyed the challenge of taking a "piece of history" and bringing it "back to life." The renovation included a 12-room addition on the back (named for former owner Major), an English tea room, roof garden, porch restaurant, the traditional dining room with cherry floors, a showroom for musicals and a private club for investors (equipped with stock exchange wires and brokerage phones).

The Arnettes and Hood have succeeded in combining traditional and new at Highlands Inn, which they describe as a New England-type inn.

The address: Box 1030, Highland, NC 28741. Telephone: (704) 526-9385.

Old Edwards Inn Highlands

Old Edwards Inn and adjoining Central House Restaurant, dating back to the Civil War, are listed on the National Register of Historic Places. The original structure was a private residence around 1878 when David Norton bought it and took in summer boarders. James and Minnie Edwards adjoined a three-story brick building in the 1930s and named the consolidation "Edwards Hotel."

Rip and Pat Benton acquired the hotel in 1980 and renovated both the frame and brick portions. The couple were experienced restorers, having converted an unused garage at St. Simons Island, Ga., into a popular restaurant and antique store called Blanche's Courtyard. In three years the Bentons opened their restored hotel in Highlands as the Old Edwards Inn and Central House Restaurant The restaurant features Southern cooking favorites and seafood specialties.

The inn's rough stone and brick facade, close to the edge of Main Street, looks across at sister Highlands Inn. A stone arch forms the entrance. Overhead a small sign reads: "21 rooms for ladies and gentlemen."

Furnished with treasures collected at estate closings, yard sales and other sources, the Old Edwards Inn projects a "capricious quality," telling guests in a subtle way that they're to have fun. A real moose head, for instance, stares from the massive fireplace in the large lobby. The front desk is an antique railway station counter. Each of the 21 rooms in Colonial theme abound with antiques, mostly old pine pieces and early American accessories. Wallpaper is of the tiny print variety and the curtains are ruffled.

The inn is opened year round. The telephone: (704) 526-5036. The address: Old Edwards Inn, 4th and Main Streets, Highlands, NC 28741.

circa 1915

Greystone Inn Lake Toxaway

Greystone Inn retains atmosphere of the private mansion once owned by Mrs. Lucy Moltz. It overlooks the 13-mile shoreline of Lake Toxaway and the distant Blue Ridge Mountains. The dining room is the same one that Mrs. Moltz dined in. The parlor was her parlor. Wicker furniture and hanging baskets adorn the sun porch like they did when Mrs. Moltz sat there. Each bedroom is still special. Early morning light bathes through walls of windows in one room. Skylights in another cast warm starglow after dark. Two bedrooms share a terrace above the lake's sapphire blue waters.

Meals are bountiful, gourmet style. Tariff includes breakfast and dinner.

The 1915-built Swiss revival house is a historical reminder of the heyday of Lake Toxaway as a resort known as "the Switzerland of America." Pullman cars, sometimes four times a day, brought wealthy families to the resort. They included the Edisons, Fords, Firestones and Dukes. Its era ended in August 1916, however, when the earthen dam broke with a roar and the artificial Lake Toxaway washed away.

A new dam, completed 45 years later in 1961, refilled the lake and its scenic beauty once again lures vacationers. To accommodate them, a parnership organized by Tim Lovelace of Brevard purchased in the 1980s the old Moltz Mansion and six chalets and a small cottage nearby in the woods. Lovelace spent nine months studying famous inns and turned the Tar Heel old-timer house into the 15-bedroom Greystone Inn. The mansion's distinctive stonework inspired the name.

The creation of Lovelace and his partners is a distinguished inn of incomparable beauty by a lakeside in the mountains.

The Greystone's address: P.O. Box 6, Lake Toxaway, NC 28747. Telephone: (704) 966-4700.

Eseeola Lodge Linville

Eseeola Lodge reflects the rustic architectural characteristic of the mountain resort of Linville. Chestnut bark covers the balsam timbered inn as well as surrounding cottages. The wood is a vestige of the great American chestnut which once dominated forests of the southern Appalachians but eventually succumbed to blight after the turn of the century.

The summer lodge, fronting the main road through the village of Linville, nestles below Grandfather Mountain. A timbered arcade connects its stone gatehouse to the lobby. Balsam railed balconies extend from second floor rooms. Stone boulders underpin the structure. A mountain stream channels beneath its underside and across the lawn. Trout dart about in the clear water of the stream.

A coterie of adjacent cottages match the main lodge. Giant evergreens soar above their roofs. Small apple trees and flower plots cluster at the base of the trees.

Eseeola's interior continues the chestnut motif with walls paneled in wood from the extinct tree. Pictures of bird and hunting scenes line the walls. Two huge stone fireplaces dominate the lounge. The effect: an atmosphere combining both ruggedness and elegance.

Formality prevails in the dining room where guests choose from such traditional house specials as pan fried brook trout or ragout of spring lamb with steamed Carolina rice, noodles and Beurre and chocolate fudge cake a la mode.

Opened as Eseeola Inn in 1892, the lodge takes its name from the Cherokee word *Eeseeog* for Linville River, meaning "river of the cliffs."

The address: Eseeola Lodge, Linville, NC 28646. Telephone: (704) 733-4311.

31

BED & BREAKFAST

The Baird House Mars Hill

Around the turn of the century the Baird House was the ruggedly handsome home of the first medical doctor in the mountain county of Madison. Folks describe it as the grandest house around. It had the deepest well (225 feet), servants quarters, a stable and two gardens. It also was the office of Dr. John Hannibal Baird and a place for locals to exchange news in the doctor's waiting room. When Dr. Baird didn't care to see anyone, Mrs. Baird refused to lie that he was away. So he named three rooms in the home for the three counties of Madison, Yancey and Buncombe where he visited on horseback. On a day he chose to hole up she would say to those who wanted to see him that he was in Madison, Yancey or Buncombe, depending on the room he happened to be in.

Dr. Baird died in the 1920s.

In 1980 his heirs sold the house to Jeanne T. Hoffman, wife of the academic vice president of Mars Hill College, who restored the home into a bed and breakfast guesthouse.

Mrs. Hoffman operated the Baird House as a bed and breakfast inn until she sold it to Yvette Wessel, who came to the inn as a guest, fell in love with the place, and bought it without a backward glance to the Connecticut she had left.

Mrs. Wessell spent many months renovating and redecorating the house. The house is now fully furnished in valuable English and French antiques, oriental rugs and original artwork. Yet, the timeless charm and warmth of this typically Southern home has been preserved.

There are 5 bedrooms for guests. Two have private bathrooms; two have usable fireplaces. Guests are invited to "sit a spell" in the book-lined living room, on the marble patio or the front porch where rockers beckon. Of course, a full breakfast is served.

The Baird Inn is open every month but December. The telephone: (704) 689-5722. The address: 121 South Main Street, Box 749, Mars Hill, NC 28754.

Snowbird Mountain Lodge Robbinsville

Perched atop a mountain far from beaten paths, Snowbird Lodge overlooks valleys and wave after wave of the Snowbird Mountain range. The "in-the-sky" retreat adjoins acres of virgin hardwood and abundant wildlife including boar and bear.

Built of native stone and timber from the now extinct chestnut tree, Snowbird Lodge is a cozy hideaway with a small 46-guest capacity in the midst of rugged Nantahala National Forest. The nearest town is Robbinsville, 12 miles away.

Stacks of cordwood and kindling flank the entrance, readily available for the large stone fireplace inside where a warm fire breaks the nip of cool mountain air.

The interior of the lodge is paneled native woods— butternut in the lounge and cherry in the dining room.

Trees surrounding the lodge, some labeled, represent the broad spectrum of species indigenous to the area. Red bud, dogwood and rhododendron especially bloom abundantly during spring. The pungent pine scents the summer air. All plant life turns into a myriad of color in autumn.

Snowbird's substantive food amply fortifies guests for ambling walks or hikes over challenging mountain trails radiating from the lodge. Guests more sedentary by nature enjoy the spacious flagstone terrace which provides a panormaic view of the mountain ridges and glimpses of sparkling Lake Santeetlah and the valley homes and fields of the Snowbird Indians.

The idea of the Snowbird Lodge was developed in the early 1940's by a Chicago travel agent, Arthur Wolfe. At that time his agency in the Windy City promoted conducted tours through the Great Smoky Mountains. Transportation was by train to Knoxville, then by bus on a seven-day scenic tour to Asheville and back to Knoxville. Needing a stopover on the return trip, Wolfe and his brother Edward selected the Snowbird site and built the lodge.

Opened in 1941, the lodge at first hosted guests largely from the Smoky Mountain excursions and travel agents in the Chicago area. Today, the lodge, operating from late April to November, attracts clientele from all parts of the country.

Bob and Connie Rhudy are the innkeepers.

The address: Snowbird Mountain Lodge, Joyce Kilmer Forest Road, Robbinsville, NC 28771. Telephone: (704) 479-3433.

The Orchard Inn Saluda

The Orchard Inn combines touches of farmhouse simplicity and Southern plantation elegance. Its nine bedrooms are decorated country style with brass beds and hand-woven rugs. The elegant dining room, a long glassed-in porch overlooking rolling peaks of the Warrior Mountain Range, serves fine food with background strains of Mozart and Schuman flowing through the room softly lit by candles on the tables.

The downstairs great room is appointed with antiques, rugs, paintings, pottery, baskets and flowers. A crackling fire in the massive fireplace nips chilled air. There are two libraries.

In 1981 Ken and Ann Hough renovated the inn on 18 acres atop Saluda rise at an elevation of 2500 feet. Views are spectacular, the air clean and the water spring fed.

Ken's background includes being headmaster of a college preparatory school in Charleston, SC. and an operatic tenor. He also is a gourmet cook and serves as the inn chef. Some of his specialties are chilled peach soup, fresh mountain trout, sweet breads and raspberry pie.

The Southern Railway Company built the two-story frame structure in the early 1900s. It provided a summer vacation home for railroad clerks until 1963.

The Orchard Inn address: Box 725, Saluda, NC 28733. Telephone: (704) 749-5471.

Melrose Inn Tryon

A good inn often improves with each change of ownership. An example is Melrose Inn of Tryon. Constructed more than 100 years ago, the building sold originally to the Charles Kenworthy family. Following Dr. Kenworthy's death, his widow operated it as a boarding house until she sold the property in 1923 to the Jervey and Baker families. They made it a lodge in 1925 for both summer and winter visitors. In 1960 the Jerveys and Bakers sold the lodge and in 1984 the David Fields, Jr., family of Charleston and Pinehurst purchased it from interim owners. The Fields redecorated the lodge and turned it into an inn. They named the rambling structure the Melrose Inn.

Now fully mature, the Melrose offers 10 rooms. Breakfast is served to overnight guest. Also available are lunch and dinner.

Good inns seldom pass away. Like the Melrose they continue and improve with time.

The address: Melrose Inn, 211 Melrose Avenue, Tryon, NC 28782. Telephone: (704) 859-9419.

Mill Farm Inn Tryon

Chicagoans Chip and Penny Kessler refurbished a stone house near Tryon into the Mill Farm Inn. The carefully assembled collection of local stone dating from 1939 sits on a 3½-acre lot. The Pacolet River flows by the rear boundary. Lovely plantings and fine landscaping abound in the setting. Bird-watching is good.

The bed and breakfast has eight bedrooms, a spacious living room with oft-glowing fireplace and sitting porches.

The Mill Farm Inn is located on NC Highway 108, 2½ miles from Interstate-26 and 1½ miles from Tryon. The country inn has a sister village inn in Tryon. It is the L'Auberge.

The address of both inns is Box 1251, Tryon, NC 28782. Telephone (704) 859-6992.

Pine Crest Inn Tryon

After 70 years as a village inn in the heart of Tryon, Pine Crest still cares for guests at the end of a tree-lined lane where " the rest of the world doesn't come." The inn with nine cottages around it provides 31 rooms, all with private baths and two-thirds with fireplaces.

The dining room seats 65 and serves three meals a day, seven days a week.

The vintage inn was started by Carter P. Brown of Michigan, a pioneer Tryon developer who helped advance fox hunting and other equestrian activities for which the village is famous.

The innkeepers today are Bob and Helene Johnson.

Pine Crest is listed in the National Register of Historic Places.

The address: P.O. Box 1030, Tryon, NC 28782. Telephone (704) 895-9135.

Mast Farm Inn Valle Crucis

The Mast Farm Inn, built in 1885, began operation as an inn in the early 1900s by Finley Mast and his wife Josephine. Aunt Josie and Uncle Finley were widely known for their hospitality and bounty of good food. According to author Elizabeth Gray Vining in her book *Quiet Pilgrimage:* "every day there appeared on the long, white-clothed table at which we all sat fried chicken, ham, homemade sausage, hot biscuits and spoon bread, homechurned butter, thick cream, cottage cheese, vegetables just out of the garden, ever-bearing strawberries, applesauce, peaches. Once I counted twenty different dishes."

In 1972 the Mast Farm entered the National Register of Historic Places as an example of a self-contained mountain homestead. In 1985 the 18-room house was restored as an inn and restaurant by Francis and Sibyl Pressly along with the two-room log cabin, the spring house, wash house, ice house, large barn, blacksmith shop and gazebo.

The inn offers 10 guestrooms tastefully decorated with mountain crafts and flowers. Rooms bear names of Mast family members, a former guest and an employee.

Breakfast is served in the dining room or in guest rooms on request. Dinner is served to overnight guests or others at either 6 or 7:45 p.m. Tuesday through Saturday. On Sunday lunch is served at 12:30 and 2:30 p.m. Diners may sit at small tables for two or four or at big tables for more persons. They help themselves from generous dishes of well-prepared fresh vegetables and salads straight from the Pressly garden.

In the early 1900s visitors escaped heat of summer and enjoyed solitude of a mountain valley at the old inn. The Masts added to this a personal touch that made guests' stays memorable. Today, more than 75 years later, guests experience the same warm feeling at the Mast Farm Inn restored and operated by Francis and Sibyl Pressly.

The address: Mast Farm Inn, Box 704, Valle Crucis, NC 28691. Telephone: (704) 963-5857. Opened May 1 to early November and December 27 to March 15.

MAST
FARM
INN
Restaurant
& Lodging

Jerry Miller

The Swag Waynesville

Guests drive 6½ miles off the nearest highway to reach The Swag Inn near Waynesville. The climb, much of it unpaved, is worth the effort. The large log building constructed in the early 1970s for Dan and Deener Matthews, an Atlanta Episcopal pastor and his wife, caps a meadow on the crest of 250 acres of a mountain above 5,000 feet. When skies are clear, Mt. Mitchell, 50 miles away and eastern America's highest, can be viewed.

Formerly, a mountaineer cultivated potatoes on the land and hauled the produce down the mountain on a mule-drawn sled. The Matthews family dismantled logs from six old structures, including a church and a 1795 cabin, and pulled them to their inn site for log building craftsman Roy Smith to erect their log cabin, "the biggest ever seen" in the county. Local masons pieced together without mortar surface rocks from dry creek beds and hillsides to form a massive rock chimney. The only deviation from log cabin authenticity is oversized windows in the living room. The Matthews wanted more light than an authentic cabin provides. The inn draws water from a spring, producing a year-long average of 12 gallons a minute at 58-degrees. The Matthews utilized three bulldozers, a dynamite crew and 150 truckloads of gravel to smooth out their 2½-mile driveway.

For 10 years the Matthews retreated to their log cabin "castle" as a private escape from Atlanta. (The Swag was built while Dan was in Knoxville as rector of St. Davids Parish. He is now rector of Trinity Parish in New York City.) In 1982 they decided to take in overnight guests and become innkeepers. For pastor Matthews, the inn became an additional "ministry." Out of their decision emerged an Appalachia gem. The Swag, a mountaineer word describing a dip in a ridge, offers 11 rooms, featuring fireplaces or wood stoves, patchwork quilts on walls and beds, and private baths. Rockers line the front porch, facing a vista of valleys far below. Swimmers may dip in the spring-fed waters of the Swag Pond. Guests are served three gourmet-style meals. Evening dinners are opened to nonguests by reservation. The telephone: (704) 926-0430. The address: Rt. 2, Box 280-A, Waynesville, NC 28786.

The Inn at Bingham School Chapel Hill

Eleven miles west of Chapel Hill at the intersection of Highway 54 and Mebane-Oaks Road, The Inn at Bingham School offers Southern hospitality in the restored home of the former headmaster of an old preparatory school. The countryplace, combining Greek Revival and Federal styles, offers six spacious bedrooms with luxurious private baths. Guests socialize in the 18th century living room and formal dining room. They roam the surrounding 10 acres of farm and woodland and enjoy a full English breakfast in an airy sun room.

Bingham School, built around 1835, served for years as a preparatory school for young men seeking entrance to The University of North Carolina. The school no longer stands but the headmaster's home has withstood the test of time. It is listed in the National Historic Registry. Hosts

Jane and Robert Kelly, formerly of Greensboro, restored the two-story frame house following retirement and in 1986 offered its unique accommodations for others to enjoy, especially former UNC alumni who revisit their alma mater. It is operated year round. The telephone: (919) 563-5583. The address: Box 267, Chapel Hill, NC 27515.

circa 1935

Carolina Inn Chapel Hill

"A cheerful inn for visitors, a town hall for the state, and a home for returning sons and daughters."

This inscription above the fireplace in the Carolina Inn aptly describes the stately lodging place at The University of North Carolina in Chapel Hill. Situated at the breast of the campus of the first state university to open its doors in America, the inn's collegiate atmosphere is unhurried. Guests relax in rocking chairs beside imposing white columns on the old "Mount Vernon" porch. Student waiters serve formally in the elegant Hill Room. Private groups meet in the Pine Club, Carolina Room, Old Well Room and the noted blue and white university ballroom. A cafeteria provides informal, quick service. On a wall at the cafeteria entrance are unusual circus scenes carved in wood several decades ago by an European immigrant.

Profits derived from the inn operation are used by the

university to support the library.

The inn's reputation for charm shows clearly in both its old and new sections. Spacious hallways, entrance ways and rooms, oriental rugs, fireplaces, colorful wallpaper and large mirrors reflect a gracious gentility.

Additions to the Carolina Inn in 1971 follow the colonial style of the original building created in 1923 by university architect Arthur C. Nash. With the 101 rooms of the initial structure plus the additional 42 built in 1971, the inn can house 350 guests. Twenty-five rooms are traditionally reserved for ambulatory patients from the campus hospital.

The inn was constructed in 1924 by John Sprunt Hill. He gave it to the university in 1935. From the beginning the inn has been a symbol of southern hospitality, warmth and ease in an academic setting.

The Fearrington Country Inn   Chapel Hill

The Fearrington House, Restaurant and Country Inn continues the heritage of the Fearrington Farm, part of the landscape between Chapel Hill and Pittsboro since the founding of America. In the 1780s the farm was a cotton and tobacco enterprise; in 1829 a magnificent farmhouse was built on it; during the Civil War and the passing era of King Cotton it declined; in 1926 a new house replaced the original which burned; in the 1930s a change to dairy farming occurred; and in 1974 Jesse Fearrington sold the farm to R.B. and Jenny Fitch of Chapel Hill.

The Fitches turned the bucolic 650-acre farm into the village of Fearrington, a special place to live, shop and dine in the countryside. The Fearrington homeplace and existing farm buildings became the village center which includes a gourmet restaurant, a Southern garden shop, a jeweler, a needlepointer, a market for gourmet foods and a pottery.

Residential neighborhoods of single family homes and townhouses are erected in the woodlands surrounding the village.

In 1986 the Fitches added a 14-room inn to the already existing Fearrington House Restaurant. Modeled after small country inns common in England and France, it is built around an enclosed courtyard. The bedrooms are furnished with antiques bought by the Fitches during several visits to England.

The couple named the combined inn and restaurant the Fearrington House, Restaurant and Country Inn.

The inn features a cooked breakfast and afternoon tea. The restaurant offers dinners and Sunday brunch. A nearby market/cafe is available for lunch.

The Fearrington House, Restaurant and Country Inn is located eight miles south of Chapel Hill on US 15-501 towards Pittsboro. The telephone: (919) 967-7770 or 542-2121. The address: The Fearrington House, Fearrington Village Center, Pittsboro, NC 27312.

The Homeplace Charlotte

The Homeplace, a country Victorian bed and breakfast in southeast Charlotte, is aptly named. For 64 years it was the homeplace of Sardis Presbyterian Church minister R.G. Miller and his family. The pastor built the two-story residence in 1902 in a rural setting. The surrounding is now urban and the Miller family no longer owns the house but its style of yesteryear remains with a wrap-around porch, rocking chairs, hand-crafted staircase, 10-foot headed ceilings, heart-of-pine floors, formal parlor, three bedrooms each with a fireplace and 2½ wooded acres.

In 1984 Peggy Dearien and her husband Frank purchased the house which was restored in 1983 and opened it to guests. Their interior decor includes paintings of primitive artwork done by her 88-year-old father, John Gentry, who began painting at age 79.

Mrs. Dearien serves a full breakfast consisting of egg/ meat dishes, homemade breads, pastries, jellies and other goodies.

The Homeplace address: 5901 Sardis Road, Charlotte, NC 28226. The telephone: (704) 365-1936.

The Morehead Inn Charlotte

Guests enjoy The Morehead Inn located only minutes from downtown Charlotte. It sits on East Morehead Street which once served the suburb of Dilworth in the heyday of streetcars. A quiet historic district with lovely oak-lined streets, handsome residences and Latta Park, Dilworth is undergoing preservation and restoration.

In 1984 The Morehead Inn became part of the revival with renovation as an inn. The former estate built in 1917 by C.C. Coddington consists of the main house and two courtyards, a carriage house and a columned veranda house. Innkeeper Nancy Bergmann named the inn for the street on which it is located. The ex-school teacher likes the name because the street namesake, the Morehead family, strongly supported public education.

Innkeeper Bergmann furnished 12 suites in the main house and carriage house with English and American antiques.

The Morehead Inn breakfast includes surprises such as strawberry bread and pumpkin muffins. There's also an elaborate Southern breakfast.

The address: 1122 E. Morehead Street, Charlotte, NC 28204. The telephone: (704) 376-3357.

Jolly Mill Restaurant Elkin

The Jolly Mill Restaurant, a three story structure built in 1896, spent 84 years as a grist mill, and the last years as an imaginative restaurant, capitalizing on the atmosphere and decor of the old mill.

The mill passed through four owners, adding additional functions with each successive owner.

The present dining room is located in a three-story structure added in 1930 to house the hammer mill operation, with grain storage bins above. One can observe grain spouts coming through the floor overhead. Dining is on two levels of the building, each room conveying a sense of intimacy and nostalgia. Both dining rooms overlook rushing water of Big Elkin Creek. A third section has been added to the original structure to house the staircase to the dining rooms, the rest rooms and kitchen.

The restaurant is usually open mid-March through January. Dinner is served Wednesday through Saturday (5:30-8:30) and a Sunday family-style lunch from 12-2 p.m.

Menu specialties include roast duckling with raspberry wine glaze, shrimp amisette and petit filet St. Jolly. Nightly specials appear on a front porch blackboard.

Lodging is not provided.

The Jolly Mill Restaurant is reached by taking Highway 21 north of Elkin for one mile, turning left on Carter Mill Road for 1½ miles, and then turning left for a short distance.

The address: Route 3, Box 126, Elkin, NC 28621. Telephone: (919) 835-7720.

The Greenwich Greensboro

A building constructed in 1895 as the first home office of Cone Mills in Greensboro serves today as a small elegant inn with English flavor in the Old Greensborough historic district.

The 28-room Greenwich features luxurious surroundings in 18th century decor. Furniture includes four-poster beds, wing chairs and chests-on-chests. A continental breakfast and champagne on arrival are served in the pine paneled lobby beside the fireplace or under the portrait of "The English Gentleman" or beneath a wood-carved deer head with antlers. Otto Zenke, well-known Tar Heel designer, decorated the downtown inn interior.

Opened year-round, the Greenwich is the closest thing to an exquisite European-style inn that can be found in North Carolina.

The address: 111 Washington Street, Greensboro, NC 27410. Telephone: (919) 272-3474.

Greenwood Greensboro

Greenwood provides bed and breakfast accommodations in Greensboro's bucolic Fisher Park three minutes from downtown. The "stick-style" house, built in 1905, is an award-winning private home for bed and breakfast in European tradition.

There are five bedrooms named for flowers—the Bluebell, Sunflower, Orchid, Dogwood and Poppy. The house overlooks the park, ideal for walking, jogging or picnicking.

Guests may enjoy a roaring fire in winter or a pool dip in summer.

A continental breakfast includes fresh orange juice, cereals, homemade muffins and bread.

Jo Ann Green is the hostess.

The Greenwood address: 205 North Park Drive, Greensboro, NC 28401. Telephone: (919) 274-6350.

The Colonial Inn Hillsborough

For over 225 years the Colonial Inn of Hillsborough has witnessed first hand the sweep of American and North Carolina history.

In 1781 Cornwallis headquartered in the inn when his British troops occupied the village. Annoyed by the muddy streets, the general ordered his men to improve the community by laying flat flagstones at the entrance of the lodge and in all directions from the intersection of King and Churton streets.

In 1796 Aaron Burr visited the inn prior to his candidacy for the vice-presidency.

In 1865 General Sherman's Union Army marched into Hillsborough. Sarah Stroud, who operated the inn, hid her daughters and hoped the soldiers would not raid the inn. The "Yankees," not so considerate, promptly began ransacking the place.

Thinking that at least one of the soldiers might be a Mason and remembering the Masonic apron of her deceased husband, Mrs. Stroud raced to a second story window and waved the garment before the troops below. A Masonic sergeant, recognizing the apron, commanded the men to return items stolen from the inn and thereafter protected the facility from further pillage.

The original facility antedates the Revolutionary War. A tavern at first, it served as Hillsborough's hospitality center during the village's wilderness days. When fire partially destroyed the tavern in 1768, the building was reconstructed as an inn. It has since served as the local meeting place for residents, political leaders and visitors.

The Colonial Inn has been described by several names.

At one time or another it was called Spencer's Tavern, Orange Hotel, Occoneechee Hotel, Corbinton Inn and Strayhorn Hotel.

Written records of the inn before 1865 are scarce. Deeds of that year, however, show that H.C. Stroud and his two brothers purchased the business. Stroud, who became Grand Master of the old Masonic Eagle Lodge Number 19 (located across the street from the inn) before leaving Hillsborough to join the Confederacy, died of influenza in 1864. He left his wife Sarah with eight young daughters. It was she who saved the inn from Sherman's troops by waving the Masonic apron.

In 1908 T.A. Corbin bought the inn and added an annex. He sold it in 1920 to H.L. Akers of Washington, D.C. In the 1950's Charles and Ann Crawford took over management, followed in the 1960's by V.V. "Pete" Thompson and his wife. In the 1980's Carolyn Welsh and her mother, Evelyn Atkins, assumed management of the historic establishment.

Atmosphere of the inn has changed little during the past 225 years. An old stone porch flush to the street, a double veranda, old plank floors, an innkeeper's desk, 11 bedrooms, a warm fire in winter and genuine hospitality create the ambience.

Complementing the setting of yesteryear, food is cooked the "old South way." Regular menu entrees include country cured ham with red eye gravy, chicken and dumplings, fried chicken, butter beans and okra.

The address: Colonial Inn, 153 West King Street, Hillsborough, NC 27278. Telephone: (919) 732-2461.

Fran's Front Porch Liberty

Fran's Front Porch near Julian and Liberty is a countryside restaurant in the family home of its namesake, Frances Causey Holt. Having inherited the homeplace from her father, Wiburforce Causey, Frances Holt and her daughter Carolyn Beyer converted in 1976 the early 20th century structure into a restaurant to help maintain the farmhouse. Today, guests at Fran's serve themselves buffet-style for dinner and sit in one of three dining rooms. When weather permits, they may dine under umbrellas on the front porch enveloping three sides of the large frame house. In spring and summer guests also enjoy flowers planted in beds around the porch and the yard. For further decor baskets of plants hang in and outside the house.

An all-meat homemade chicken pie is the house specialty. Other entrees include roast beef, countrystyle steak, stuffed peppers and pork chops and baked ham. Fran's homemade yeast rolls and 20 various cakes and pies, all baked by Fran and her two daughters Carolyn Beyer and Sylvia Belvin, add to the offerings. No alcoholic beverages are served.

Fran's Front Porch operates year-round except for two weeks at Christmas. The evening meal is served Thursdays, Fridays and Saturdays from 5 to 8:30. Sunday lunch is from noon to 2:30.

Fran and her two daughters compiled a cookbook, *The Best in Southern Cooking;* it sells at the Front Porch.

The restaurant, which offers no lodging, is located off Highway 62 on Smithwood Road directly across from Causey Aviation. The telephone: (919) 685-4104. The address: 6139 Smithwood Road, Liberty, NC 27298.

Pine Ridge Inn Mount Airy

An imposing white mansion with a large swimming pool built in 1948 as a private residence five miles west of Mount Airy was converted in 1984 to a bed and breakfast inn. Appropriately named Pine Ridge Inn, it overlooks pine covered foothills of the Blue Ridge Mountains and is near Exit 100 of Interstate Highway 77.

The hosts, Ellen and Manford Haxton, members of the original family who owned the colonial-style home, serve a Southern continental breakfast. In addition, luncheon and dinner (gourmet-type) are available by reservation.

There are six bedrooms.

Visitors find Mount Airy an interesting small city. Famous residents have included Eng and Chang Bunker (the Siamese Twins), Andy Griffith and Donna Fargo. It is home of the world's largest open faced granite quarry and within sight of distinctive Pilot Mountain.

The telephone: (919) 789-5034. The address: 2893 West Pine Street, Mount Airy, NC 27030.

circa 1900

Holly Inn Pinehurst

Holly Inn, a Pinehurst landmark since 1895, underwent restoration in 1985 and now caters to modern "carriage trade" as it did to yesteryear "carriage folks."

The historic beauty on the village green was constructed of hand-hewn long leaf pine. The 14- by 18-inch thick pine beams in the clapboard and brick structure are so sturdy that they need no reinforcement after nearly 100 years.

Heart of the inn is Tufts Lounge, an octagonal room with a tentlike ceiling. The paneled walls are curly pine, a vanishing variety. Each panel has a different kind of curl or wave in its grain.

The lounge is named for Pinehurst's founder, James Walker Tufts, a successful Boston manufacturer, who built the New England-style village in the once barren sandhills of North Carolina.

The old mahogany-paneled "Dutch Room" is now the "Victorian Dining Room." As the main dining room, it features skylights and polished wainscoting extending to the cupola 20 feet above.

Each of the 79 rooms and suites is different, a special place for rest unlike any other.

The address: Holly Inn, Pinehurst, NC 28374. Telephone: (919) 295-2300.

The Manor Inn Pinehurst

The 1923 white stucco Manor Inn retains pleasantries seldom experienced by guests nowadays. A doorman parks bicycles of guests on return from excursions over lanes of Pinehurst, a Southern landscaped filigree of dogwoods, pines and magnolias. Rockers line the Manor's porch where simple sitting is enjoyed for its own sake. While they sit, guests sip the inn's "iced tea."

In 1983 the Manor remodeled and added a new look—"the Greens." The glass-walled room with skylights and fireplace features an informal dining room and viewing grill-kitchen.

Dinner is a grand matter at the inn with six courses selected from a rotating menu. The entrees split almost even between classic French dishes and American fare (fried chicken and baked ham are favorites).

The 50-room Manor represents "country in tradition" with as much elegance and old-time amenities as any inn.

Its address: Magnolia Road, P.O. Box 1479, Pinehurst, NC 28374. Telephone: (919) 295-6176.

Angus Barn Raleigh

The Angus Barn is a barn indeed—Tar Heel style. In 1959 the creators of the "beef eaters' haven," Thad Eure, Jr., and Charles M. Winston, instructed architects to draw the barn first, then insert the floor plan. Atmosphere was to be as important to Eure and Winston as food quality. They wanted their gourmet creation to reflect the surroundings of a rustic barn symbolizing the rural way of life in North Carolina, an agricultural state historically.

The result: An Angus Barn evening is a fascinating "country museum" experience as well as a culinary delight. Construction materials and furnishings in the Barn represent as fine a collection of rural North Carolina memorabilia as can be found. The nostalgic pieces include a millstone from Johnston County's Moccasin Creek; cobblestones from old Raleigh streets; fireplace brick from the capital city's long vanished Giersch's Cafe; timber from the ante-bellum residence of Governor Thomas Bragg; and harnesses, oxen yokes and wagon wheels from farms here and there in the Old North State.

Rounding out the establishment's country decor are actual barn catwalks and lofts used as dining areas on the second floor. Hay racks divide spacious booths; private dining rooms are stables; mule muzzlers are wall vases; and horse collars and tobacco hands are decorative pieces which hang from the pine walls.

Outside the big red barn, a windmill, dismantled from an old Virginia plantation, whirls among wind-swaying pines.

Deriving its name from Angus cattle, its food specialty, the Angus Barn annually serves over 160 tons of prime aged beef to customers who have continued to increase in number since the facility opened in 1960. The meat is cooked over 5,000 pounds of charcoal each week. Diners receive their beef on heated cast iron skillets resting on wooden platters. Over 300 beef-eaters can be seated at once; 1,500 served within a single evening.

The beef comes from far western states—mostly from Nebraska. Chefs charcoal all types and sizes of cuts before the eyes of guests. Rib eye steak accounts for half of the orders. Prime rib is popular but available only on Tuesday and Thursday.

Waitresses serve in checked gingham dresses to look like milkmaids.

The Angus, a one-meal-per-day operation, serves only in the evening. The facility is located on a bluff overlooking the Raleigh-Durham Highway at the airport turnoff. Its address: Box 6357, Raleigh, NC 27628. Telephone: (919) 787-3505.

The Oakwood Inn Raleigh

The Oakwood Inn, a lavender and gray Victorian beauty, rises from the crest of a small hill shaded by giant oaks amid Raleigh's historic Oakwood district. The State Capitol and Governor's Mansion are within strolling distance.

White wicker armchairs scatter across the wide front porch. Formal velvet, porcelain and mahogany luxury exudes inside the rambling six-bedroom mansion. An ornate brass and mahogany grandfather clock greets guests in the entrance hall. A 300-year-old Chinese Imperial bed with a mahogany canopy of 2,000 inlaid pieces of ivory and wood in one bedroom beckons sleepers. At almost every turn whimsical cherub faces stare out from brass chandeliers and mahogany armoires. Truly extraordinary is the collection of Oriental, Eastlake, Empire and Victorian antiques in the inn.

Guests are treated to a lace-napkin Southern breakfast including homemade breads, fruit, cheese and meat casseroles.

The inn opened in 1984, the creation of four Victorian romantics and collectors—Chris Yetter, Steve Zamporelli and Donna and Oakley Herring. In 1987 Diana J. Newton and three friends bought the inn. Ms. Newton serves as the innkeeper.

For years the inn had been the "old Rayner-Stronach house." It was built in 1871 by Kenneth Rayner, a delegate to the North Carolina Constitutional Convention of 1835. For 30 or 40 years the A.B. Stronach family lived in it. By the 1970s the dwelling had become a boarding house.

Once the new owners decided to convert the house to a bed and breakfast inn, they invested heavily in designing, renovating and antique furnishing the old house to renew it as a "true sense of place." The current owners are equally committed to the authentic turn-of-the century ambience of the inn so that fortunate travelers can experience Victorian splendor in downtown Raleigh for the price of an evening stay.

The Oakwood address: 411 North Bloodworth Street, Raleigh, NC 27604. Telephone: (919) 832-9712.

Brookstown Inn Winston-Salem

Brookstown Inn, a 40-room hostelry created within the walls of an 1830's cotton mill, features a decor combining an eclectic blend of sparse 17th and 18th century primitivism with 20th century "industrial chic" concepts. Each spacious room has a unique shape with loft ceilings, often including exposed handmade brick walls, rough-hewn beams and columns, fireplaces and windows at unexpected places and angles.

Rich fabrics and Appalachian handmade quilts appear throughout the bed and breakfast inn from the elegant parlor to the most secluded guest room tucked under the building's eaves. Guests enjoy old world ambience, while luxurating in a modern spa bath. In the antique-filled parlor duirng the evening they further enjoy house wine accompanied by a "bit of brie." In the dining room during morning they experience a continental breakfast featuring home-baked Moravian sugar cake and Love Feast buns. The delicacies are served on elegant china and linen table cloths. The Irish cupboard in the dining room displays a collection of antique pewter, blown-blue porcelains and teapots.

The inn's history extends back to 1752 when Moravians from Pennsylvania founded a religious settlement in the North Carolina wilderness and in 1766 established the town of Salem. In 1836 the church board discussed establishment of a modern cotton factory in Salem. Thirty stockholders subscribed $50,000 and machinery was ordered from Baltimore.

In 1837 Salem Cotton Manufacturing Company began operations under Superintendent Francis Levin Fries. In 1854 Governor John Motley Morehead of Greensboro bought the factory. In 1863 he resold it to Fries. In 1880 Fries added to the mill and renamed it Arista. It was the first factory in the South to be lit by electricity. In 1964, following restoration and listing in the National Registry of Historic Places, Brookstown Mill became a complex consisting of specialty shops, a restaurant and the 40-room bed and breakfast Brookstown Inn.

The inn is located in Winston-Salem at 200 Brookstown Avenue, between the bustling commercial center of Winston and the restored colonial village of Old Salem. The telephone: (919) 725-1120.

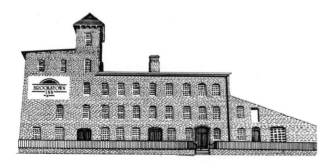

Salem Tavern Dining Rooms Winston-Salem

Moravian chicken pie, beef ragout, rack of lamb, deviled duck, pumpkin muffins, ginger bread and amaretto chocolate pie headline the menu in the annex of a Winston-Salem tavern built in 1816 by the Moravians, a devout Germanic people. The annex is called the Salem Tavern Dining Rooms.

In their initial plans for the community of Salem, the Moravians assigned a high priority to a tavern. If Salem were to be a trading center in the rugged back country of piedmont Carolina, it was essential that there be a lodging place for passing travelers and traders who would buy wares of the skilled Moravian craftsmen. A tavern would also generate income to help defray community expenses, the practical-minded Brethren calculated.

By 1772 the tavern and other basic buildings of Salem were completed. The tavern's reputation quickly grew with travelers journeying extra miles to enjoy its homelike comforts. Fire, however, destroyed the half-timber building in 1784. So important had been the tavern to the community that residents within five days had cleared the ruins and begun another building—this one of brick. Still standing, the 1784 tavern is designated a Registered National Historic Landmark.

The tavern's good food and hospitality continued to bring such success that by 1816 an adjacent building was constructed to accommodate the overflow of guests. It is this weatherboarded annex which now serves as the Salem Tavern Dining Rooms.

The annex, a major building in the restored Old Salem complex, features six dining rooms on two floors, four of which have fireplaces. The furnishings and decor reflect early 19th century style. Some of the pieces were made in Salem at that time, for example, the cupboard in the lower hall and the clock on the stair landing. The tables are Old Salem reproductions and the "butterfly" sconces are copies of a local Moravian design.

To complement the decor, tables in the Salem Tavern Dining Rooms are set with such items as pewter service plates, plain glassware, linen napkins, pottery ashtrays and off-white candles in brass holders.

Evening light is provided by the candles. Waiters and waitresses dress in early Moravian attire.

All breads and desserts come from the tavern kitchen. Dark beer and hot spiced apple cider are available.

Lodging is not offered.

The address: Salem Tavern Dining Rooms, 736 South Main Street, Winston-Salem, NC 27101. Telephone: (919) 748-8585.

Zevely House Winston-Salem

The Zevely House represents the handiwork of a Moravian cabinetmaker, Van Neman Zevely. He built the structure in 1815-16 on a 160-acre plantation near Winston-Salem where he conducted a wool carding operation.

In 1974 the dwelling was moved to its present location and fully restored as a restaurant. The site is the 900 block of West Fourth, the main street of Winston-Salem. The house, the oldest dwelling standing in what was known as Winston township, is at a location where the business district ends and the old residential section begins.

Food at the Zevely House is American-Continental. The management does not serve strictly Moravian or colonial dishes because it does not have authentic records of those recipes.

The house chefs, however, feel the menu is appropriate to the period. All cooking is done from scratch and fresh vegetables are used as they were in colonial days.

The offerings include daily specials representing all the meats—seafood, beef, veal, chicken, lamb and game birds.

No lodging is provided.

The Zevely House address: 901 West Fourth Street, Winston-Salem, NC 27101. Telephone: (919) 725-6666.

Colonel Ludlow House Winston-Salem

The Colonel Ludlow House aims at a specialized guest market with discriminating taste for luxurious quarters. Owner H. Kenneth Land provides these in an 1887-built Queen Anne-style house with stained glass windows. It is furnished from top to bottom with antiques in an air of under-stated elegance.

The parlor, with 12-foot ceilings and triple 10-foot windows, features an 1852 square grand rosewood piano, a Victorian settee upholstered in gold velvet and lace curtains on the windows.

The ten guest rooms accentuate detail. The brass and iron bedstead in one bedroom, for example, is covered with eyelet-trimmed sheets and a crocheted spread made from tobacco twine. A lawyer's bookcase contains reading materials. The front bedroom has an armoire with lace curtains near the foot of the bed concealing a whirlpool tub.

For a romantic bed-and-breakfast hideaway with charm, the Colonel Ludlow House, named for the original owner, may satisfy the most discriminating guest.

The address: Corner of Summit and W. 5th Streets, Winston-Salem, NC 27101. Telephone: (919) 777-1887.

63

Tanglewood Manor House Winston-Salem

Tanglewood Manor House exemplifies the creation of a fine inn from the estate of a wealthy family passed on. The conversion preserves a valued homeplace for family descendents and offers ordinary citizens a sampling of the life style of yesteryear's rich.

Millionaire William N. Reynolds and his wife Kate B. built their home in the traditional manor concept of a large house surrounded by extensive land. The colonial structure centers a 1,117-acre estate along the Yadkin River in the rolling hills of piedmont North Carolina. Reynolds named the layout Tanglewood. Abounding in woods, it represented his dream of sylvan luxury.

Tobacco money made possible the dream. Reynolds came from the Winston-Salem family which pioneered the manufacture of tobacco products, such as the most popular cigarette ever made in America—the "Camel." In 1954 the Tanglewood estate, including the Manor House, was opened to visitors. Will and Kate Reynolds, in a magnificent gift, had provided North Carolina one of the finest parks and recreation areas in the country.

Guests at the Manor House sleep in the same bedrooms of colonial decor; eat Conish hen and other delicacies in the same dining room; and relax in the same elegant parlor as did the Reynolds' family.

For further sampling of Tanglewood style of "good living" guests may stroll to nearby stables for horseback riding, play tennis and golf on fine facilities, fish and browse through a formal rose garden.

They also may hike the vast woods and explore interesting places on the grand Tanglewood estate. There are, to mention a few places, a deer park, a big barn now used as a summer stock theatre, an old church dating back to 1819, the Yadkin River where Daniel Boone once hunted and several lakes bearing such colorful names as Mallard, Skilpot and Coon.

Such a *modus vivendi* is rarely available in this age of franchised accommodation facilities.

The address of the Tanglewood Manor House, located off Highway 158 west of Winston-Salem, is Box 1040, Clemmons, NC 27012. Telephone: (919) 766-0593.

The Jenkins House Restaurant Ahoskie

The Jenkins House Restaurant caters to oyster and other succulent seafood lovers in the Roanoke-Chowan River lowlands centered by Ahoskie. The area has more than its share of seafood devotees. To capitalize on their craving, Hugh Johnson III created The Jenkins House Restaurant. It represents the placement of a unique seafood eating establishment with oyster bar in an atmosphere full of Eastern North Carolina flavor. Johnson would have been pressed to find a site with more flavor. The vintage Jenkins House was erected in 1770 as part of a cotton plantation, remained in the Jenkins family possession until 1965 and survives as the oldest family dwelling in Ahoskie. Johnson also saw the restaurant itself as a place of flavor, and a little history, where one's child, grandchild or great-grandchild could sample a "plump, juicy oyster."

The restoration of Jenkins House required months of painstaking planning and rebuilding. Hand-hewn beams and flooring, fireplaces and wainscoting were retained as they were 200 years ago. The high chimney will "draw the hat off your head—it really works." Even some of the original shingles from the kitchen remain on the dividing wall between the dining areas. The wainscoting is made from over 50 doors, some coming from old Halifax tenant homes, some from a Rich Square school, circa 1922. The stained glass windows are from an old church that burned in Wilmington. A beautiful door separating the dining areas actually came from the Joe Jenkins family in Colerain.

Founder Hugh Johnson III no longer is in the area but the Jenkins House heritage he instigated is carried on and has been built upon by Jim, Evans, and Jamie Johnson and manager, John Taylor.

The Jenkins House Restaurant serves Tuesday through Sunday. There is no lodging. The telephone is: (919) 332-6346. The address: Jernigan Swamp Road, Ahoskie, NC 27910.

The Captain's Quarters Beaufort

The Captain's Quarters represents the effort of a retired Michigan airline captain and his family to make a turn-of-the-century home into a "museum of the Victorian era."

In 1985 Dick Collins (flew 38 years as a United Airlines pilot), his wife Ruby, daughter Polly and a crew of workers restored and filled with Victorian antiques and reproductions an old Beaufort home. They even painted the front porch ceiling sky blue to make the house a Victorian summer home by the sea.

As a bed-and-"biscuit," it offers three guest bedrooms. One room features double iron beds fronting a fireplace.

When The Captain's Quarters first opened, Dick Collins announced in the soothing voice of a former airline pilot, "We are ready for people to come on board."

The address: 315 Ann Street, Beaufort, NC. The telephone: (919) 728-7711.

The Cedars at Beaufort Beaufort

The Cedars is a small country inn in the historic and house-proud seaport town of Beaufort. The building (circa 1768), representative of coastal-colonial architecture, was built as a summer home by a Rhode Island shipwright who had settled in nearby Mill Creek.

In 1985 the structure was lovingly restored as an inn by Suzin Osburn and her husband. It features four guest suites with antiques and fireplaces. There also are rocking-chair porches.

Breakfast and dinner are served to inn guests only. The menu reflects a blend of classical French and new American ingredients: fish from the nearby Gulf Stream, specially grown vegetables, herbs from The Cedars' gardens, shellfish, fowl and game. Appetizers include smoked fish and oysters. True American snapper and pan-roasted quail are additional popular entrees.

A sunfish sailing dinghy, waterski boat, sunset harbor tours and picnics on Carrot Island are available for guests.

The Cedars' address: 305 Front Street, Beaufort, NC. Telephone: (919) 728-7036.

River Forest Manor Belhaven

River Forest Manor, a cosmopolitan inn in a provincial setting, has catered to guests as distinguished as millionaire Harvey Firestone and stars James Cagney, Talullah Bankhead and Twiggy. Its architecture is Victorian, featuring huge porches, Corinthian columns, a ballroom, walls of tapestry, a mahogany-paneled dining room and crystal chandeliers. Its cuisine encompasses delectable foods served buffet style on a three-tiered table. Its location: Belhaven, in remote coastal North Carolina.

Representing colorful tidewater towns, Belhaven borders the Pungo River. It is a port for shrimp boats, center for crabmeat processing and site of a boatworks. It is a prosperous, quaint town but hardly large enough (3,000 population) to support an inn of such style as the River Forest Manor.

The Intracoastal Waterway explains the presence of famous and wealthy people. Enroute north and south in seagoing yachts, they slip into Belhaven's little harbor for fueling and berthing for night.

River Forest Manor, in its Victorian hauteur, crouches on a green lawn overlooking the coffee-colored waters of the Pungo, which for several miles comprises a segment of the inland waterway. The inn's marina services the passing yachts and the dining room lures the "sailors" aboard to its buffet smorgasbord. The spread features local crabmeat, scallops, soft shell crab and homecooked vegetables, as well as pies, cakes and breads prepared by the inn's veteran cooks.

River Forest Manor was opened in 1947 by Axson Smith, a Tar Heel who grew up in Belhaven where his father owned the old Carolina Hotel. It was a labor of love for Smith to convert the Manor from an old colonial mansion.

Belhaven began as a lumber town, and the mansion was built in 1904 by John Aaron Wilkinson, the president of the John L. Roper Lumber Company and vice president of the Norfolk Southern Railroad. After his company cut the timber from the coastal land, Wilkinson planned to sell the cleared acreage for settlement. He conceived grand ideas of land promotion, and used the showy mansion to entertain and impress midwestern farmers and others to whom he hoped to sell real estate.

Eight years after its completion, the mansion became the domicile of Wilkinson and his wife, a New Yorker. They shared the dwelling for years. At Wilkinson's death, the house was sold to J.W. Hines of Rocky Mount.

Axson Smith, who trained at some of Chicago's fine hostelries—the Drake and the Palmer House—returned to Belhaven following World War II, bought the Wilkinson mansion, utilized his experience and established the River Forest Manor.

The institution continues operation under Smith's widow, Melba, and his son, Axson, Jr., as "Smith has gone to that great inn in the sky but his spirit thrives in the historical mansion he converted to a hostelry."

The River Forest address: Box 219, Belhaven, NC 27810. Telephone: (919) 943-2151.

The Lords Proprietors' Inn Edenton

Edenton, nestled on a bay near the head of Albemarle Sound, is as beautiful as any little town could be. Its charm can especially be appreciated from The Lords Proprietors' Inn. The inn comprises three beautifully restored homes adjacent to one another on Broad Street in Edenton's historic district. Together, the three homes offer guests 17 spacious bedrooms, each elegantly appointed with antique furnishings. The mahogany beds, many with canopies, have all been made by a local cabinet maker and may be reproduced for guests.

On the brick patio behind the middle house stands the newly-built Whedbee House dining room, where the innkeeper serves breakfast. All breads and preserves are homemade.

Jane and Arch Edwards opened the inn in 1980. They settled in Edenton after 18 years of living in cities around the world. Before opening the inn, they restored their own home, Mt. Auburn, c. 1800, a beautiful place in an incredible setting. Guests are invited to swim in the large pool overlooking the river and on certain nights may enjoy a cocktail cruise on the Edwards' pontoon boat.

The address of The Lords Proprietors' Inn is 300 North Broad Street, Edenton, NC 27932. Telephone: (919) 482-3641.

Station Six Restaurant Kitty Hawk

Station Six Restaurant occupies the Old Kitty Hawk Beach Lifesaving Station. The gourmet enterprise combines seafood dining and the preservation of a beloved historic landmark.

The Gothic designed lifesaving station, one of seven built in 1874 on the North Carolina coast, was constructed with cypress lumber shipped from the mainland.

The surfmen who manned the station were a breed apart, "reared in the tradition of the sea and master of the oar ... They knew that, no matter how turbulent the sea, regulations required that they go out. They went willingly, knowing that regulations said nothing about coming back, and that might be their fate."

In 1903 the weather station in the building furnished the Wright brothers with temperature and wind velocity readings for use in their airplane flight experiments and sent out over its wires news of the first successful flight.

In 1947 when the Coast Guard decommissioned the obsolete lifesaving station, the property reverted to heirs of the original owner and the "grand old lady" went up for sale. It served successively as a gift shop, office facility and inn until winter storms eroded away the beach and the building sat almost at water edge.

In 1985 new owners Cecil Bryan and Mimi Adams bought the aged structure that had been moved across the road to a safer location and opened the "Station Six Restaurant," offering lunch and dinner daily. In preserving the landmark, they rendered a distinct public service.

The address: Station Six Restaurant, corner of Kitty Hawk Village Road and U.S. 158 Business, Beach Road Mile Post 4, Kitty Hawk, NC. Telephone: (919) 261-7337.

The Dill House Morehead City

The Dill House was home of the late George Dill, mayor of Morehead City for 27 years. Captain Rick Yarling and his wife Carol operate it today as an inn with three guest rooms. The home is decorated in a combination of contemporary wicker and antique furnishings. Oriental rugs spread over refinished oak floors. In winter a crackling fire burns in both the dining and living room fireplaces. And there is even a player piano with over 75 rolls from which to choose.

Breakfast, served on fine china in the formal dining room, consists of fresh fruit, juice, blueberry pancakes with hot maple syrup, bacon, sausage and cheese omelets with toast and jam.

No guest reportedly leaves the Dill House without a bag of Mrs. Yarling's homemade chocolate chip cookies. It took her "years to perfect the recipe."

The Dill House, located downtown, is within walking distance of the waterfront, restaurants and unique shops. The address is 1104 Arendell Street, Morehead City, NC 28577. The telephone: (919) 726-4449.

Winborne House
1840

Winborne House Murfreesboro

The Winborne House hosts guests in a restored mid-1800s home in a small college (Chowan College) town which once bustled as a riverport of the Old South. Docks at the boat landing on the Meherrin River are gone but the lazy stream still curves by Murfreesboro and the town retains its "Old Southern" rural charm. The Winborne House and over 100 mansions and other structures of pre-Civil War vintage have been restored. Locals garden in vacant spaces wherever they find good soil; some plots are mainstreet backlots.

In this setting Winborne guests may relax on the front porch, walk among tall pines in a quiet place, enjoy flowers (daffodils are especially pretty in mid-March), socialize over a continental breakfast and tour the town.

Two bedrooms are available in the Winborne House hosted by Innkeepers Edna and Dick Hammel, a warm and friendly couple. He is a retired Army officer. Their address: 333 Jay Trail, Murfreesboro, NC 27855. Telephone: (919) 398-5224.

Henderson House New Bern

Tryon Palace visitors and local residents enjoy gourmet dining in the elegant Henderson House. The brick, center-hall Federal House is listed in the National Register of Historic Places as the Hatch-Washington House for two early owners. When David and Alyce Faye Grant opened the inn in 1973 they chose to call it Henderson House in honor of the last family to live in it as a private residence.

Luncheon is served daily Tuesday through Saturday and dinner Thursday through Saturday. Southern peanut and cold peach and plum soups are menu specialties. They set off broiled crabmeat on English muffin and shrimp and chicken salad. Other selections include prime rib, scallops, lobster and lamb with all homemade desserts prepared under supervision of owner/chef Matthew Weaver.

Chef Weaver and his parents purchased the Henderson House in 1983. The father had retired as Professor Emeritus of Indiana University where he taught art for 34 years. As did the Grants, the Weavers operate the inn as a family.

Diners enjoy paintings of Mr. Weaver featured in the dining rooms along with antique furnishings. They may also enjoy the art gallery on the second floor.

The original deed for the property on which the Henderson House presently stands was recorded on February 17, 1749. The Town of New Bern sold to Elias Lagadere for 40 shillings "one good habitable house and lands."

Dr. Thomas Haslen, purchaser of the property in 1779, was a mayor of New Bern, a businessman of substance and a Loyalist which caused him to flee with a bounty of 5,000 pounds on his head. The Haslen family played a distinct role in the social and business life of New Bern until they fell on hard times and their property was sold to Durant Hatch in 1817.

The Henderson House address: 216 Pollock Street, New Bern, NC 28560. Telephone: (919) 637-4784. No lodging.

King's Arms New Bern

Three couples wanted to do something about visitors who tour Tryon Palace in New Bern, then leave town to sleep elsewhere. So in 1980 they turned an aged Pollock Street house into a colonial inn. They named it King's Arms after an old New Bern tavern, said to have hosted members of the First Continental Congress. "The idea was to offer people a place to stay on one of New Bern's most historic blocks."

The couples, the Walter Paramores, John Petersons and John Thomases, rotated duty as innkeepers every third weekend. At times they considered it less duty than fun.

In 1986 David and Diana Parks bought the inn and continued its operation as the innkeepers.

King's Arms has eight plush rooms. Individually decorated with canopied and poster beds and antiques, they provide a homey setting. Homebaked breakfasts are served in the rooms.

The inn represents old New Bern. John Alexander Meadows, a turpentine distiller and shipyard owner, built it in 1847. His daughter Mary sold it to Mrs. Harriet Green in 1871. She in turn sold it to Mayor Hahn several years later. In 1978 Mrs. Sarah Bradbury converted the dwelling into an antique shop-residence.

David and Diana Parks now retain it as an inn featuring an unusually deep "bell cast" mansard roof with gabled dormers in the warm colonial atmosphere of New Bern.

The address: 212 Pollock Street, New Bern, NC 28560. Telephone: (919) 638-4409.

The Island Inn Ocracoke

The Island Inn offers food and lodging to visitors of Ocracoke Island, the southern-most segment of the Outerbanks reached by public ferry or airplane (3,000-foot runway). Thirty-six rooms, some furnished with antiques, are available. Menu specials include prime rib, crab cakes, broiled seafood platter and oyster omelette.

The history of the inn dates back to 1901 when it began as an Odd Fellows Lodge and a school (the ground floor). During the 1930s the property was sold as a private residence and was moved across the road to its present site.

In 1941 native Ocracokan R.S. Wahab bought the place and converted it into an inn. His nephew Larry P. Williams helped operate the facility. After the Navy established a base on the island during World War II, the inn became an officers club.

Subsequent owners following the war added to the inn and in 1976 Williams, who had left the island and returned, and Foy J. Shaw bought the establishment and refurbished it greatly. Williams had completed 21 years teaching English at a Virginia Beach high school and Shaw had been teaching psychology at a Chesapeake, Va. community college.

The Island Inn address: Box 9, Ocracoke, NC 27960. Telephone: (919) 928-4351.

The Tar Heel Inn Oriental

Although located in a riverside village named Oriental, The Tar Heel Inn reflects an English country inn atmosphere. Within its enclosed grounds are a brick patio and courtyard and an English garden. Its six bedrooms, each decorated using Laura Ashley prints, feature king- or queen-size fourposter or canopy beds.

There is little Oriental about Oriental but there is much nautical about it. Water borders the community, lying at the confluence of the Neuse River and Pamilico Sound. Sailing ranks foremost among year-round activities of residents and visitors. Fresh- and salt-water fishing is second.

Converted from a turn-of-the-century home, The Tar Heel Inn began operation in 1984. It had been restored to an intimate bed and breakfast inn to the last minute detail by Dr. and Mrs. Eugene Hodgson. Owners-Innkeepers Harry and Frances Edwards manage it with equal detail for comfort and pleasure of guests. The telephone: (919) 249-1078. Address: 205 Church Street, P.O. Box 176, Oriental, NC 28571.

French Country Inn Selma

The French Country Inn, located in a turn-of-the century home on a quiet residential street in Selma, features a fixed menu of courses from a specific French province. The menu remains the same for two weeks and then changes to reflect dishes typical of another province. All food is produced from prime, fresh and seasonal ingredients and all courses, including the breads and pastries, come from the inn's own kitchen.

The provincial representation often includes cuisine with overtones beyond the French border. Some of the provinces, for example, lie adjacent to Spain, Italy and Germany and the influence of these countries is detectable in the food.

Provincial cuisine at the French Country Inn is just that—food eaten by local people in France and not found in fancy restaurants of Paris. This does not mean that it lacks fancifulness. During the period that the food of the province of Bordeaux was featured, for example, the menu consisted of pate de crevettes (Fresh shrimp, butter, spices and herbs enhanced by a dry sherry), tourin bordelais (onion soup), salade de tomates (marinaded tomatoes) fricandeau de veau poulangere (roast of fresh veal with glazed carrots and potato) and oeufs a la Forman (dessert, an illusionary creation of the chef).

The French Country Inn is an expression of the philosophy of the founder, Phillip Forman, regarding the preparation and serving of French cuisine. Forman, a pharmaceutical salesman for 22 years, retired early to open the restaurant in Selma. His knowledge of French cooking stems from a "35-year-avocation, almost an obsession."

Forman learned by visiting outstanding restaurants in New York, New Orleans' French Quarter and elsewhere. He experimented at home to individualize dishes he liked.

The inn is opened to 40 diners only. There is no lodging.

The French Country Inn blends into a row of old houses that line the Selma railroad tracks. The exterior setting is not French but it is definitely quaint, relaxing and provincial. The address: 309 West Railroad Street, Box 325, Selma, NC 27576. Telephone: (919) 965-5229.

Anderson House Wilmington

Connie and Landon Anderson bought the 135-year-old Willard House in Wilmington's Historic District in 1977. The house is unique in many aspects, but it has only two bedrooms so the Andersons who have three children erected the Guest House in 1981 in the garden. The addition provides two extra bedrooms, each with private bath, and are rented as bed-and-breakfast accommodations. Visitors also enjoy a tour of the main house and see the parquet floors, extensive cherry woodwork, stained glass and all the original gas/electric lighting fixtures.

The Andersons designed the cottage with private entrances to the two guest rooms. Matching the main house, the yellow stucco building appears like old servants' quarters. The bedrooms contain antique furnishings including wicker chairs, ceiling fans, footed bathtubs and a working fireplace.

Breakfast, served on the piazza overlooking the garden on warm days and in the vaulted main dining room of the house on cooler mornings, consists of a menu which might include crepes with a New Orleans cream sauce, big pancakes, blueberry cobbler, eggs Mornay or eggs Florentine. In any case, Mrs. Anderson is a "great cook."

The address: 520 Orange Street, Wilmington, North Carolina 28401. Telephone: (919) 343-8128.

Graystone House Wilmington

Graystone Guest House conveys the style of a European bed and breakfast. The four-story Italian Renaissance mansion contains 16,000 square feet of magnificently detailed interiors, including a large drawing room, ball room, music room, sitting room and solid mahogany library. Each of the six bedrooms offers "luxury and elegance of a setting much like the Astors and Vanderbilts would have enjoyed."

Built in 1905 at the corner of Third and Dock Streets on a buff above the Cape Fear River, the mansion was the home of Elizabeth Haywood Bridgers and other members of the Bridgers family until 1943. Following 40 years of various uses, the structure caught the eye of two Raleigh interior designers, Rodney G. Perry and D. Gordon Plummer. In 1983 they bought and renovated the stunning graystone landmark into a guest house in Wilmington's historic district. The area is a "charming blend of commerce, old homes, brick streets and river smells."

Guests enjoy a continental breakfast served in each bedroom on silver and fine china.

The Graystone address: 100 South Third Street, Wilmington, NC 28401. The telephone: (919) 762-0358.

Murchison House Wilmington

The Murchison House represents a Wilmington lodging alternative. Located in the historic district of the old seaport on the Cape Fear River, the house was completed in 1876 by David R. Murchison and his wife Lucy Wright. Architecture is modified Victorian Gothic. The structure's rear faces onto a formal garden and courtyard. A carriage house on the south side predates the house.

Antiques, parquet floors and many fireplaces lend charm and warmth to the interior. Especially cozy is the large missionoak paneled library. All woodwork and trim reflect Chippendale influence.

The dining room is the site of a daily country breakfast. Resident host is Joe P. Curry. The address: 305 S. Third Street, Wilmington, NC 28401. Telephone: (919) 343-8580.

About the Artists and Author

PHILIP MOOSE illustrated inns located in the mountain and piedmont regions of North Carolina which appeared in the first edition of this volume. The cover drawing of Highlands Inn before its renovation in 1986 is a Moose sketch. The drawing of the present Highlands Inn and inns not in the first edition are by other artists.

Moose, winner of Pulitzer and Tiffany Awards, lives in a rustic house overlooking Grandfather Mountain near Blowing Rock. Here he produced much of the work that won him such artistic recognition as purchase awards from six major American art museums and the British Colchester Museum; general exhibitions by the New York Metropolitan Museum and a West German museum; and one man shows on both U.S. coasts and in more than 25 North Carolina museums, galleries and colleges. Although widely known as the artist of the Appalachian Mountains, Moose does not confine his work to any one locale. He has traveled widely. On a Fulbright Award he visited Germany in 1953 and Taiwan in 1963. He went around the world in 1967 and spent 1972 in the South Pacific.

The Blowing Rock artist trained in seven schools, including the Academy of Fine Arts in Munich, Germany; Taxco (Mexico) School of Art; and Columbia University. He was an associate professor of fine arts at Davidson College (1951-53) and Queens College (1956-67).

KATE RUSSELL FORBES lives in Salem, Virginia, where she is a free-lance artist. Her work is primarily woodcuts and tapestry with drawings of Victorian Houses a favorite sideline. She holds an associate degree from Stephens College (Columbia, Mo.) and a bachelor's degree with a major in studio art from the University of North Carolina at Chapel Hill.

FARIS JANE COREY explored for the original edition over 25 country inns in North Carolina extending from the Island Inn on the Outer Banks in the Atlantic Ocean to the Snowbird Mountain Lodge in the Appalachians. With assistance by her parents, she has added 41 inns across the state for this revised edition. The revision is the fourth publication on a North Carolina subject by Ms. Corey. The three others are *Exploring the Mountains of North Carolina*, *Exploring the Villages of North Carolina*, and *North Carolina Superlatives*.

The books have become a tradition with the Corey family whose members possess a keen interest in their home state. Writing about its finer things is a family avocation.

The Tar Heel earned a bachelor's degree at the University of North Carolina at Chapel Hill and a master's in language and reading development at the University of California at Berkeley. She studied one summer at Oxford University in England through a UNC English and philosophy program. She taught English for three years in Charlotte, N.C. and Trona, Calif. public schools. Since then she has served as an officer in banks in Charlotte and Jacksonville, Fla.